ONE HAPPY
DIVORCE

HOLD THE
BULLS#!T

Jennifer Hurvitz Weintraub

ISBN: 978-1-943258-54-3

Edited by: Jenny Kanevsky
        Amy Ashby

Published by Warren Publishing, Inc.
Charlotte, NC
www.warrenpublishing.net
Printed in the United States

For Jonah and Zac: The reason I never give up.
And for Mark: The reason I'm "Happily Divorced."
I love you all to the moon and back.

Introduction

FIRST OF ALL, NO ONE WANTS TO GET DIVORCED.

You're not walking down the aisle, planning the end before it begins. No one whispers to the rabbi, "See ya at my next wedding," or, "Is this a buy one, get the next free?" Yeesh. We all go in hoping for the best!

Let me give it to you straight, OK? (Are you holding onto your panties?) Statistics show more than 52% of all marriages now end in divorce. So, maybe you should be worried. Maybe it *is* a good idea to approach the chuppah with trepidation. What? Too negative for your Martha Stewart sensibility? Fine then, put me down. Go on, drop my ass. I'm not for everyone; I tell it like it is. I don't sugar coat shit, y'all. Willy Wonka, I am not. This book is for truth seekers only.

So, are you in?

Then listen up.

I'M NOT BEING PESSIMISTIC, I'M BEING REALISTIC.

With over half of all marriages headed to splitsville, I know it's sad, I know you're mad, but don't be a baby. I can show you how to do it right. The kind way, the way it should be done. Drama-free, stress-free, and as simple as possible. And if kids are involved, the *only* way — happily! Children should be a game changer.

LOOK AT THOSE KIDS, AND REMEMBER TO ACT LIKE GROWN-UPS!

Easier said than done. But divorce doesn't have to be a disaster or destructive.

Work on one thing... Get happy.

I am happily divorced. I did it. Whoop whoop! I know, it's not easy, it *wasn't* easy. But you can do it, with work — and wine! Keep reading with an open mind and you will get there. And, I can help.

Trust me.
What do you have to lose?

KIDS FIRST, DUH!

I REALLY DIDN'T GET IT AFTER THE SEPARATION.

WERE WE SUPPOSED TO SWEAR AT EACH OTHER AT CARPOOL? SAY HORRIFIC THINGS AND ROLL OUR EYES?

MAYBE GIVE EACH OTHER THE SILENT TREATMENT OR FLIP EACH OTHER OFF AND MAKE EVERYONE ELSE FEEL UNCOMFORTABLE?

WHAT WAS THE NORM FOR DIVORCED COUPLES THESE DAYS?

didn't *feel* normal let alone understand what normal looked like. My girlfriends couldn't look at me and most of Mark's friends didn't call to see if he was OK. I lost my marriage, and was about to lose my kids for *half of their lives*. Half of their lives. I wanted to puke. I was moving out of our family home and moving into an apartment with my ex.

Wait, what?

Let me explain.

We were "*nesting*" for a few months so the boys could adjust to the separation. You see, "nesting" was all the rage in 2013. It's when the kids stay in the family house, and the parents get an apartment. Yes, *the same apartment.* (No, they don't share bedrooms.) Then the adults, as caregivers, move back and forth from the family home. The kids don't have to go anywhere. They never pack a bag or a toothbrush. They never leave their dogs. Or their beds. It's kind of amazing if you think about it. I know, it's a little unconventional, maybe. But hear me out. It's the new thing, and, it's amazing, and selfless.

It was the most selfless thing I ever did in my life. I put my kids first, 100%. This was not like, oh, you get the first donut, or sure, go ahead, name the flippin' dog. No. I mean, putting them totally and completely first. Got it?

And pay attention now:

YOU HAVE TO BE READY TO GIVE UP YOUR LIFE TO MAKE "NESTING" HAPPEN.

It's no picnic. In fact, it's a fucking nightmare. Imagine this, OK? You live in a two-bedroom, two-bath apartment with your new ex, the person you now cannot stand in every conceivable way. You hate the way they chew! When they clear their throat you want to kill them. And you alternate weeks. In and out. Packing your stuff every Monday. Can you imagine that? My clothes, and shoes, even my underwear, (which he did not get to see anymore, thank you very much). I had to remember everything, and then for the work week, what would I need? I couldn't forget one little thing. And we'd see each other in passing, try to be civil, touch base with each other about how the kids were doing, make sure the kids were adjusting, try to avoid any bodily harm and throat clearing. Not easy, I'm telling you.

GOING BACK AND FORTH EVERY OTHER WEEK, MOVING ALL YOUR STUFF, SCHLEPPING, AND SWITCHING BEDS, UGH!

Think about that.

You big dummies. This swapping is exactly what your kids do every time they switch houses! **Nesting is putting yourself in your kids' shoes.** We got a taste of what they would eventually face, moving between our two houses. Packing a suitcase and changing settings. New sheets, different smells and sounds, one parent instead of two. Their special belongings, things they only had one of like their blankies and stuffed animals. I remember my little guy telling me, "It's the only thing the same between both houses, and it smells like you, Mom." He was talking about his plush rabbit and he held onto that thing tighter than ever. *It smelled like me.* I'm sobbing as I'm typing this.

He still has that rabbit. Sometimes, he makes me sleep with it so it can get the "smell back."

So, nesting was a complete clusterfuck. I did it for my boys so they could see how it would feel to be alone with each parent. A pseudo-separation period. Make sense? It made sense to us; putting our kids first. And that my friends, is how being *happily divorced* begins.

"HAPPILY DIVORCED" BEGINS BY RECOGNIZING THAT YOUR CHILDREN COME FIRST. THEY DID NOT ASK FOR THIS SEPARATION. THEY DID NOT CHOOSE A DIVORCE, YOU DID.

Plain and simple. So if you can do that, and mean it, then keep reading. If not, then set this book aside and read it later, when you're ready. You'll get there. Come back to it. Being happily married takes effort, so does being happily divorced. That's the mantra, y'all.

I love those people that say, "Oh, my kids are fine going back and forth. They love the 2-2-5 schedule. It's so easy; they are great with it." Really? Have you tried it? Give it a shot. Go on, go! Set yourself up in an apartment, and then go back and forth to another place on a 2-2-5 schedule. Then add homework and sports. Throw in your work, and dance. Grocery shopping. Feeding the dogs. Then, have someone "forget" something back at the ex's house. Yup. That's about how "easy" it is for your kids. Try it. Then, get back to me.

Oh, what's a 2-2-5, you ask? Ha, silly me, well it's really more of a 2-2-5-5 and it goes like this: Each parent has two set weeknights and the weekends rotate. Your kids spend two weeknights with you and the next two weeknights with the other parent. They then come back to your house and spend three weekend nights and the first two weeknights you are assigned, equaling five nights. Guess what's next? They go back to the other parent and have their two assigned nights along with the three weekend nights, again equaling five nights. Known as a 2-2-5, or 2-2-5-5. Completely simple, right? *Wrong.* It's crazy. Here's what it might look like in picture form. I think it's nutso.

Sun	Mon	Tues	Weds	Thurs	Fri	Sat
Parent A	6 pm switch	B	6 pm switch	A	6 pm switch	B
Parent B	B	B	6 pm switch	A	A	A

For parents, it's easy, you have assigned weeknights. Some claim it is more consistent. More consistent than what?

Look, I never said reading this book would be easy, but I did promise the truth. I nested and went between two houses bi-weekly for six months. I know exactly what your kids are feeling. And, I'm sorry to drop the bomb, but it's anything but "great." And sure, they are resilient. And yes, they get used to it. And of course, two houses are all part of a divorce. But if you could make the transition easier, wouldn't you? (Rhetorical.)

Am I saying that nesting is for everyone? Hell no. If you can't get along with your ex for a second and the divorce is wicked nasty then nesting is not good for your kids. It's not healthy, and it is better for your entire family to separate and move on quickly. Or, if you don't have the financial means to support two places, then it is what it is. Nesting is only an option if it works for your family. Do what works for you; don't make an already stressful situation worse. But, consider it. Please. For the kids.

Mark and I continued to nest as long as we could. We lasted six months before we lost our flipping minds. At that point, the boys understood the why and how of things. We were all ready to separate and move forward with our lives. Apart – but together. Two different houses, two different families, one set of parents. Just co-parenting in different places.

See, we have this!

You with me?

I HATE HIM

I HATE MY EX. I MEAN I REALLY HATE HIM.
I CAN'T STAND TO LOOK AT HIM.
OR BE IN THE SAME ROOM WITH HIM.

want to shake him and say, "Do you know how much I want to slap the living shit out of you?" I want to jump up and down and yell, "Clean up your shit, I don't work for you anymore!"

Ok, whoa. Remember what I said earlier. Nesting is hard, but it is worth it for the kids.

Read on, y'all.

See, I'm referring to the part of nesting where all four of us were living in the same place. Not together, but overlapping. Ya, that. He would come over and hang out to watch a game, or have dinner and leave his empty cans on the coffee table. Or he'd leave his fucking dishes on the counter. Or better yet, make gross-ass sliders and leave the mess (for me to clean). Then he'd be off to the apartment and it was my week. Or every once in awhile, he'd stop by to say "Hi" (super-sweet!).

But he'd open a UPS package and leave deserted packing peanuts all over the floor, the dog would eat them, choke, and puke. *He'd leave dog puke.* Then I'd step in it.

And fuck my life.

And fuck him!

I got so angry. We'd yell at each other and scream. And Zac would say, "Ladies! To your corners!" Even he knew better; no fighting in front of the kids. Never, ever, ever. So, until we could get our shit together, we'd take a break from each other in the nest. It wasn't healthy for the boys — or for us.

It's important to check yourselves. Go to your corners until you can come out with gloves off. No arguing in front of the kids (same rules as when you were married). Take it outside, or via text where little ears can't hear you. Nothing is that important. And remember, your kids are a part of your ex. You may be not be blood-related to him, but they are. And don't you ever forget it. So, when you decide to bad-mouth him in front of those kids, who are you actually bad-mouthing? *Ahhhh, yes.* Check it!

WE MADE RULES:

- NEVER FIGHT IN FRONT OF THE KIDS.
- NEVER MAKE THEM CHOOSE ONE PARENT OVER THE OTHER.
- NEVER BAD-MOUTH EACH OTHER.
- NEVER PLAY THE VICTIM OR THE HERO.

After a little breather, (OK, months of breathing), we can hang out as a foursome, and it's a good thing. Usually. To be together as a family, it's a great thing, actually, but that is only if and when we get along. And get along we do! We fare better than when we were living under the same roof. Or sharing spaces, "nesting." We have set up a workable living situation. We each have our own homes. We do the change-up every Friday night after school, which allows the boys the weekend to get adjusted and in order in case anything is forgotten before the next week begins. And then we're all good and ready to go.

As for me, I spend less time yelling at Mark and more time texting him to remember to bring Jonah's this or Zac's that. I don't clean up after Mark anymore. And I realized something huge: *I am not married to him anymore.* I am no longer his wife or his friend. I am his co-parent. We are two people raising our children together. We are better than we were, and it takes time.

Time, understanding, and patience.

And look, I'm not here to judge anyone else for their choices. But my answer to all of this is simple: put your kids first. As far as divorce goes, my kids didn't ask for it. They didn't walk into our bedroom one night and say, "Hey Mom, I think you and Dad should end this sham of a marriage. It sucks, and we want out." I mean, can you imagine? They didn't want this shit. What they did expect was a happy, loving family with two married, in-love parents living in the same house. Maybe a white picket fence and a couple of goldfish. Or a puppy. They wanted family trips and holidays together. They wanted their mom and dad together. They wanted to be *happy*.

And guess what? We screwed that up. We did. I'm not gonna lie, or pretend we didn't. I wish I could take it back, rewind the clock, undo this mess I made, but it's done. Sure,

I'm a better parent now than I ever was married. But, can I explain that to a ten-year-old? Not yet. Maybe someday I can sit them down and tell them how I wanted to see fireworks when I kissed the right person. And how I wanted to be "in love" with my soulmate. *Fuck.* How can a child understand that now, in their little heads, in their little lives? They can't, and it's not OK to expect them to. It's not. Mark and I shattered their expectations of what a "real family" was supposed to be; we stole that dream. I don't really think I'm a good mom; I am sad every day for taking that "perfect dream" away from them. But I also know if you ask them today, they would say they are happy and well-adjusted.

I hope that's the truth; so, I believe it.

So, for now, the least I can do is give them the best divorce — the best of the worst. I will put me first when they can live on their own and don't need me anymore. Does that make sense at all? It should. For now, I will do what's best for them. My boys. My breath and my soul.

Since my kids come first, getting divorced was important for them, too. Happy parents equal happy kids. I am happy knowing I do the best I can each day. Except for today. I admit, today, I wanted to kill them. And up my meds. And call my therapist for an emergency appointment. Ha! Or drop them on their dad's front porch. "Yo, Mark! It's your turn to parent! I'm *done* like dinner! These two are all yours!" How's that for the truth?

Today, I hated my ex-husband. And I wanted to kill my kids.

But Mom always says, "Tomorrow is another day."

MAYBE I WON'T FEEL LIKE KILLING ANYONE.

MY VERY OWN PB&J

SO, I HAVE A NEW HOUSE.

AND IT'S MY NEW HOUSE.

OH, AND IT'S MY PEANUT BUTTER SANDWICH.

Remember that? Anyone? It's from *St. Elmo's Fire.* OK, I'm dating myself but remember that 80s movie the one with the scuba-suit wearing chick? She said the peanut butter sandwich she made in *her* house, with *her* peanut butter and jelly was *the best PB&J sandwich ever?* Right before she lost her virginity to Rob Lowe. That's me. Without the scuba suit. And I am hardly a virgin. But you get the analogy, right? I am *single and strong!* And I moved into my first house since the divorce. I also love peanut butter and jelly.

I have a new lease on life. It's my turn to do this thing. Cue the music, in the words of the late, great Whitney Houston, "I'm every woman!" I have a fucking theme song in my head and I am ready to go. Yes! Just like Ally McBeal.

Ugh. What a crock of shit.

I'M EXHAUSTED.

Sure, I'm starting over. And sure, I get to do things my way now. I get to do what I want when I want, but I'm going through a divorce while trying to hold my shit together for my kids and I'm fucking emotionally drained. I'm tired, I'm old, and I'm sad. I spent the last week packing up my life. Well, our life. After nesting for six months, I packed my things in boxes. And bags. And more boxes. I drove back and forth, and back and forth, schlepping the memories of the last thirteen years, to my new house.

MY NEW HOUSE.

Not the beautiful house where I made a home for my children and husband, but a rental house half the size. I'm not complaining; I wanted the smaller house. I let Mark keep the family house, and I'm moving out. I know, it sounds wrong. My parents were upset, too. They really felt strongly that I should stay in the bigger house. (Not like it's any of their business.) But yes, they want what's best for me. And sure, "best" always looks bigger. Thanks, guys, I'm good. But I can't afford that house. And we wanted the boys to have their home. One of us needs to stay there!

Let Mark make those huge mortgage payments. Let him take care of those monthly bills, the landscaping. I'm going to a smaller house; it's good. Just right for me, and the boys. It's perfect for us. I mean, who needs all that house (5,800 square feet to be exact)? It's only two weeks a month, and the rest of the time they'll will be with me. And the other two, well, I'll be alone. Yikes. Alone. Yes, the smaller house is perfect for me. Mark and I are of course co-parenting; it's week-on, week-off.

OMG. I just freaked myself out.

I only get them for *half of their lives.*

I took down the family pictures and put them into boxes. The ones of all of us, me, Mark, and the boys, for when they're older and want to see them later in life. Maybe they'll want to show their wives or kids? I mean, do I throw them out? No, I can't. I put away my wedding album and my videos. My ketubah is still up. (A "ketubah" is a Jewish marriage contract, but it's not just a piece of paper, it's like art and most people display them.) What do you do with it? Yikes. I sat on the bed and looked at the empty closet that I shared with Mark. I looked at all the dust bunnies — and it hit me.

MY FAMILY IS OVER. DONE. KAPUT.

I'm not sad my marriage is over. I need to make that clear. My marriage was me and Mark. We are better friends now than we have ever been. In fact, most divorced couples would kill for a relationship like ours. We had to get divorced to be where we are today. But I am sad about the family I left behind. The memories, the idea, the life. It hurt to pack up and leave it all empty. The house. The rooms. The stupid little stuff, like the drawer in the bathroom where I kept my blow dryer. What will the boys do when they need my blow dryer? Isn't that dumb? But now, it's gone. And I've left them an empty drawer. Being divorced didn't upset me. It was the empty drawer.

IT'S NOT THE MARRIAGE PART.
IT'S THE FAMILY PART.
IT'S TIME TO MAKE NEW MEMORIES.

Time to take pictures of new things and hang them on my new walls, in my new house. In my new life. With my new family. No pressure, guys, really. I'm a big girl, I can handle just about anything. And so what if it's been 12 years since I've screwed in a light bulb, I put in four all by myself yesterday! I even picked out the right kind at Target. (But first, I sat in the light bulb aisle sobbing, so many choices!) And I know how to use a hammer. Hmmm, I don't own a hammer, but when I get one, I can definitely use it.

AND IF I CAN'T, I WILL LEARN.

I will learn how to do new things. Things I never thought I'd be able to do on my own. But I will do them, because I can. And the truth is, I could do them when I was married, it just wasn't part of my "job." Plunging toilets, cleaning the garage, taking out the trash, the "dad-type" things will now be all my job, and I got this! And the boys will help me, when they're with me. It's the "alone" weeks that make me nervous.

IT'S GOING TO TAKE SOME SERIOUS GETTING USED TO.

So, that's where I am. Buying new sheets and new rugs and decorating with a vengeance. The boys love their new rooms: Detroit Tigers for Zac, Portland Trailblazers for Jonah. Listen, I'll give them the moon at this point. The guilt of this whole thing is eating me alive. But I have two amazing men in my life, Jonah and Zac. Wait, three. Mark. He is the best ex-husband, really. This can't be easy for him, either. I mean, he's now a full-time dad. Can you even imagine that? Having to do all the "mom shit" he never had to do?

Even though the divorce isn't final, I'm dating this great guy, who helped me move in. Crazy, right? He and Mark moved us in *together*, and even shared stories about me over a beer. I can't ask for anything better than that, right? It's all pretty cool. We realize we have to get along for the kids. Poor kiddos watching their things being packed and unpacked into two separate places. What have we done to them? But, it is so much easier when everyone gets along. It's good, until it's not sometimes. It ebbs and flows. But to be happily divorced takes effort. Everyone needs to be in it to win it.

So now I'm here in my new kitchen, searching for the peanut butter. Where is that bread? Jonah! Zac! Who wants a peanut butter and jelly sandwich? Well, forget them. I'm totally hungry. And I could use a glass of wine to go with it! If I could only remember where I packed the corkscrew.

IT MAID ME FEEL BETTER

I HATE BEING ALONE.

THERE, I SAID IT.

IT MADE ME FEEL BETTER.

I HAVE NO SHAME.

I can't believe I actually went to Mark's house on *my* "off-week" and did three loads of laundry, cleaned the boys' rooms, and organized his pantry.

Let me explain before you freak out.

I was *lonely*. And sad, and truth be told, I missed my "day job." I missed being a stay-at-home-mom (SAHM, that's me, baby), dammit. I missed doing my thing! Head-of-household, y'all. Shit! So I got up and I left my perfectly-perfect house and went over to Mark's shithole. Sorry, my sweet ex, but it was a shithole. Granted, he was new at this "single-parenting" thing it was still flat-out gross.

YOU HAVE TO REMEMBER, SOME DADS ARE NEW AT BEING MOMS (IN THE TRADITIONAL STAY-AT-HOME-MOM KIND OF WAY). MY EX NOT ONLY HAD A FULL-TIME JOB, BUT AFTER OUR DIVORCE, HE WAS A FULL-TIME DAD, TOO.

I felt like he needed me. *He needed me.* And I liked being needed. Dammit. I missed being needed. So, I cleaned it. I know, it was wrong. On so many levels. My shrink told me I was bad. I got a big old slap on the wrist for that one, but come on! I had to do it. I felt better, for a few hours, doing what I do best. I felt needed. And I organized the boys' closets. And I did the laundry. And I cleaned out the drawers. And boy-oh-boy, did I feel good. Like a quick hit off a snuck cigarette, it felt good. A rush of happy. A jolt of energy. Ah, but it never lasts.

My work was done, and I got ready to leave.

But not before I sat staring at my kids' baby pictures, sobbing. I hit rock bottom, cried for twenty minutes, stole a few boxes of tissues from Mark, and left. So, not only was I a loser, I was also a thief. Good times.

I went home, to *my house,* and got into bed. And realized I was alone again, with not a thing left to do. No laundry, no dishes, nothing messy to pick up. My OCD pantry was insane — labeled and color-coded. Nothing to do but wait, until it was time to pick the boys up from school.

Oh, I left that out, didn't I? Convenient of me. Even though Mark and I alternate weeks, I was still the "nanny" so to speak. I saw my guys every single day! How kickass is *that*? Put that in your settlement and smoke it! It's the best of both worlds, Mommas. Listen carefully, OK?

I SAW MY BOYS EVERY SINGLE DAY.
BECAUSE I COULDN'T BREATHE IF I DIDN'T.

I pick up my guys every day after school, and they stay with me until Mark gets home from work. For us, it's a win-win. Rather than daycare, or a babysitter, or an after school program, I'm the child care!

Some of you might not think this is so great. Some might think I'm not getting equal free time. Or, that Mark is taking advantage me. Honestly, though? I think *I* win. I see my boys every day. And that, my friends, was perfect in my book. How was that possible you ask? Because Mark and I were friends. We were able to communicate about pick-up arrangements. We texted all day long about where the kids needed to be. Sometimes, I'd have to take a kid to the orthodontist and he'd need to drive one to baseball practice. Whatever! The kids came first. And we'd talk without fighting. It was easy. If you can't be nice to each other, the "nanny thing" can't happen, so don't bother. And definitely don't do it if you'll resent your ex. Do it if you want to see your kids every day, and if you can be friendly, flexible, and can communicate effectively.

Anyway, I digress, I was home alone, and I realized it was so dang quiet. I looked at *my* house, my new house, and thought, *wow, it's cute.* I'm super proud of it. And it's clean, and just the right size for us. Really, it is. But it's missing a couple things. A couple of pretty important things.

JONAH AND ZAC.

I realized that nesting was selfless. And it was hard, sure. And it worked while it worked. Mark and I did it as long as we could. But, surprisingly, I missed it. I would do it again in a heartbeat. It was the best transition for the boys. And after six months, it was time to get separate places.

Eventually I realized what the real problem was. When I was in the apartment alone, I didn't miss anything. The boys' stuff was never at the apartment, they were never there. But in my house, *they* were missing. Make sense? I was there and they were not. Their rooms were empty; there were clothes, and shoes, but they were gone. Fuck. This was the worst. This house was too quiet and I wanted them back. I wanted noise and talking. And fighting. And the "busy." I liked the busy that came with it all.

I WANTED MY FAMILY BACK.

I used to leave them with their dad and dogs. And now, they left me. Yeesh.

Zac and Jonah, and me: we're a team. The three of us. In *my* house, with my OCD pantry and my ever-so-perfect closets. And I wanted to have a job from 8 am to 3 pm that got my ass out of bed. I had a life before I got divorced. Do you know how hard it is to get out of bed when there is *no reason to get up in the morning?* I mean, why get up? What is the point? I needed a life. A job. A career. Every other week, I needed a reason to get up! I used to be stronger. And motivated, and I needed to get that girl back.

I NEEDED TO FIND JEN AGAIN.
MAYBE START WRITING A BOOK – OR A BLOG.
OR A SITCOM ABOUT MY CRAZY-ASS LIFE.

It was my time, baby. (And by the way, I apologized to Mark for invading his pig sty that day, so you know.) I texted him right after and apologized up and down for making it all clean and pretty. I said it was for me and not for him. I said, "Thank you so much for letting me have the opportunity to make the disgusting place you call home livable again." You know what he said? That he would appreciate it if I wouldn't rearrange his things so he can't find them. *Really?* How about a thank you? What a shit. Jeez, that's the last time I ever clean his house for free. Next time, I am totally going to charge him. Then I'll be the nanny and the maid. Ha!

BE FRIENDS FIRST

SO, I HAVE THIS BLOG.

ITS NAME IS KINDA CATCHY.

THE TRUTH HURVITZ.

A LITTLE PLAY ON WORDS, GET IT?

Well, my maiden name is Hurvitz. Now, do you get it? The truth hurts. The Truth Hurvitz? Yes!

I started my blog when I got separated to have a place for my feelings. Cool, right? I wrote anything I wanted. Were there repercussions? Yes. Did people look at me differently? Whatever. Ask me if I cared? People talked about me behind my back. *But they did that before the blog.* At least they had something juicy to talk about. Ha! Certain friends wouldn't make eye contact anymore. And sure, guys were scared to ask me out because I might write about them. One guy had his attorney ready. OMG. *Really?* Like you're that important. Bring it, dude. The truth is, if you do something shitty enough that you need a lawyer, you deserve to be written about.

Look, it is what it is. I did what I wanted and said what I wanted and continued to blog about it. And why? Because it felt fucking good. And do I really need to swear? Not really, but studies show that people who use obscenities have higher IQs. Yup. The researchers at Marist College in New York say a big vocabulary of curse words is a sign of higher rhetorical skill, and those who can name the most swear words in one minute tend to have a greater overall vocabulary *(Huffington Post)*. So, there!

Look, releasing my inner-most feelings makes me feel better. That is huge. Once, I had a reader comment on my Facebook page that she wasn't going to "read me" anymore because of my language. And couldn't I "stop using the F-word?" Hmmm. I thought about it for all of three seconds, before writing back, "No, I can't. And if you don't like it, don't read me." Jesus Christ, Lady! It's a word. *Fuck.* And actually, it is a good one. A verb, a noun, and an adjective. Love it. I fucking do. (I think that was a adverb. Right? An adverb.)

I will stay in this *blogship* until it feels wrong. Or brings out the ugly in me. Or until it makes me feel bad about myself. Or until I don't like who I am when I'm doing it. Or, like certain friendships, we drift apart. Or realize we're not working anymore, our values have changed.... Where am I going with this? Stay with me people, OK?

FRIENDSHIPS. CONNECTIONS. YET ANOTHER PART OF MY LIFE THAT HAS DRAMATICALLY CHANGED SINCE MY DIVORCE.

Ok, so friendships have nothing to do with blogging. Or do they? My readers are my friends. Or were. I gained new friends. Blogging is a way for me to connect with others, so a blogship is like a friendship. It is a way of connecting. Or losing connection: because there is. so. much. vulnerability. in. blogging. So, it's an analogy teetering on shaky ground, but stay with me. No matter what, blogging impacted my friendships, for better or worse, and my friendships have completely changed since my marriage fell apart. I want to scream. And cry. And yell.

WHERE THE FUCK ARE YOU PEOPLE? WHERE HAVE YOU BEEN FOR THE LAST NINE MONTHS — WHILE I'VE BEEN SOBBING IN MY CAR AFTER SCHOOL DROP-OFF?

Was I not a good enough friend or person for you to come to my rescue like I came to yours? I needed you. I need you *now*. I am sad. And lonely. And I look OK every day, but I'm not. And I want to talk. I want to talk to you. I miss you. And us. I lost my husband. And my family. And now, I lost *you*, too?

IS LOSING A FRIENDSHIP LIKE A DIVORCE, OR IS IT WORSE?

If I could make a billboard for all separated people, it would read:

"I NEED A FRIEND. I LOOK FINE, BUT I AM NOT OK!"

Am I right? Especially, those with kids. Are we going to walk around blubbering with snot running down our faces? Come on, people. We have to hold our shit together, at least in public. It's for the kids! Like most people, when something horrific happens, we take note of those who don't show up, rather than counting the amazing friends who do, which is sad. Why do we do that? Is it because we are so angry and so hurt that we want to hold onto that pain? I could still list those people, "friends," in my head who never called me after my divorce. And I was still angry — and hurt.

MAYBE IT WAS ME?

Nah, it couldn't have been me. OK, let's say for a second that it was. Maybe being divorced is unacceptable. Or, it's not who these women want to be when they "grow up," and it's contagious! Or maybe divorced women can't do "married things." Or play housewife, or go to couple's nights. They didn't want me without a plus one; it made everything "uneven." I mean, no one likes an odd number, right? And it hurt to show up to an event where the table name was the "Flying Solos." I went to my kids' school auction and there was a "Flying Solos" table. What the fuck? Why don't they just take a knife and stab it into my heart?

Funny thing, I met a guy that night. He was sitting next to me, he too was a Flying Solo "loser." So you see, it ain't that bad, really... and you're not alone even though you're solo. You're just surrounded by a slew of other Flying Solos. Perfect. So perfect that I haven't been back to the auction since.

When I think back to when *my* girlfriends got divorced, before me, was I a mean bitch? Did I exclude them because they didn't have a hubby? No. I fucking did not. But hey, that's me. I guess everyone is different. And what if my friends' husbands don't want them hanging around a divorced chick? I could be a bad influence or a temptation. A two-bit ho! *All* divorcees are sluts. Yuppers. Rumor around town. *Sigh.* I'll have to get over it and move on.

I GUESS I HAVE TO FIND NEW BEST FRIENDS; SINGLE BEST FRIENDS.

I miss them; my girls. They were my friends who loved me when I was married, and now they avoid me like the plague. But unlike my marriage, I didn't want my friendships to end. I didn't do anything wrong, or choose it, or get to discuss it. One day I noticed certain people "fell" out of my life. Poof. Vanished like me being separated from Mark was the ultimate disgrace. Geez, girls. Are you uncomfortable – or don't know what to say? Were you worried I was too upset to talk? Why didn't you try it? Just call. Or you're jealous I made it out, and you're still in your marriages? You were miserable, sad, and lonely, and I was, well, happy? Shit, ladies! First, don't judge me for getting out. And I won't judge you for staying in. Second, don't think this is a cake walk. We all make choices. It takes a strong woman to know when to pull the plug. Mark and I were both smart enough to know we deserved happiness, we were brave. But it's also brave to stay. And it's hard work to make a marriage work. I get it! This is a judge-free zone.

JUST COME BACK.

I'm the same me, minus a husband.

And so you know, it's OK to *not* be married. Over twenty-six million people in the US aren't. (I asked Siri — and she knows everything.) Wake up and smell the divorce rate. I'm getting T-shirts made: *"Happy Divorce is the New Black."*

THE LITTLE THINGS

MY HEAD WAS SPINNING AND TO BE PERFECTLY
HONEST, I WANTED TO SCREAM AND CRY.
I WANTED TO TAKE MY LIFE, PUT IT IN A SNOW GLOBE,
AND SHAKE THE LIVING SHIT OUT OF IT.

You know, those snow globes you get at airports with little cities and landmarks inside like Times Square or the Eiffel Tower? They are so pretty and perfect, even after you shake them. Upside-down, round and round. The snow flies everywhere, it settles, and it's back to perfect.

My kids collect them. In every city Mark traveled, he brought one home for each kid. Jonah has a wicked-cool collection, and Zac, well he doesn't care. I dated a guy in DC once, so I brought one from there. I carried it carefully, convinced Jonah had to have it for his collection. It was the White House. I searched all over the airport. I am the best mom, I thought. I may have fucked up his life, but I will not go home without a snow globe. And Zac, well, I got him an

"I Heart DC" shot glass. He loved it. Started "shooting" lemonade immediately. Mom of the Year, for sure.

But when I gave the snow globe to Jonah, he looked at it, and then me. And I knew exactly what he was thinking. And even at eleven years old, he used his filters. He didn't want to hurt my feelings, but we both knew. It wasn't from his dad. And the snow globe collection wasn't at our house. So why would I get him one? Fuck. Mom of the Year is right. Maybe I thought he could start a new collection at my new house, so he wouldn't miss his other one? Or maybe a little piece of me wanted to be "Fun Mom" that brings home the snow globes?

IT'S THE LITTLE THINGS.

It's the little things. The traditions. The Thanksgiving turkey-shaped butter, and the stupid snow globes. That's what I miss about being married. Sharing a home. The holidays. The table set with an empty chair. I set a place for Mark in case he showed up. Not because I missed him, or wanted him back, but maybe because he kind of belonged. I set a place for Mark. I mean, what the fuck was I thinking? I knew he was alone. He had nowhere to go, for God's sake! I invited him, he said "no." Why did I do it?

During that first Thanksgiving after the divorce, my mom asked me why there was an empty place setting. I told her it was for Elijah and she should open the front door. We both laughed. I poured another glass of wine and put my Whole Foods pre-cooked turkey in the oven. Don't judge. You know damn well this Jewish bitch doesn't cook shit. But damn can I cater! My dad was great; he helped with everything Mark used to do. I wished my family would move here to be with me. It was the best week ever. My boys were happy, I was happy. I was so damn happy, I ate every carb I could find. I remember that day well. My first Thanksgiving as a divorcee.

It just had to get better.

My sister and I spent the week laughing, and not like you laugh at a dumb joke. No. We laughed until our sides hurt. Until we almost couldn't breathe. Until we thought we were going to pee in our pants. We laughed the way you wish you could laugh with everyone all the time, but you can't and you don't. We laughed so loud at The Palm, the lady in the next booth asked to join in the fun! And Dave, Julie's husband, he let us laugh. Mark never let us laugh. He was always so serious. He thought I was stupid. And silly. It was the first time in so long that I felt really, truly happy. And forgot about my divorce. And my kids. And my fucked up, lonely life. I was living in the moment, knowing it would end in a few days. And it did. And after living in Charlotte for five years, you would think it would get easier, right? Saying goodbye to my family.

But it didn't.

And it never will; I cry every time they leave. I am telling you, it fucking sucks. And being here in Charlotte with no one sucks. And I'm not asking for a pity party. Put away the invites and the balloons. I was just having a little Post-Party Letdown. Don't y'all have that after a huge event? Ya know, PPLD? It's a real thing!

If you had asked me five years ago where I would be today, I would I not have seen myself in Charlotte, far from extended family, no real career, and divorced. *Yikes.*

BUT HEY, LET'S SHAKE UP THAT SNOW GLOBE, SHALL WE?

My life is in there, along with the backdrop a killer skyline of Uptown Charlotte and we shake the shit out of it, the snow settles, and it's perfect. What do we see? I have amazing friends. And the best school in the world for my boys. And they play outside all the time! I mean, can you get better weather? They survived the first year of a divorce and come out OK. Mark and I are friends. He has a great job, so we live a great lifestyle. I am good to go! I have a wonderful life here, and a great place to visit home in Detroit. I am free to come and go whenever I want. I can always go home, and my family can always come here. Life is good. And most importantly, my boys are thriving. Sure, they miss their cousins and grandparents, but they love their friends here. Sounds like a perfect snow globe to me, no?

A really perfect snow globe.

So, while there will be times I get shook up, and snow flies all around me, and I'll feel lonely, sad, and angry, I know this is my home. And now, I have to let go of the past and make new traditions. I'll stop setting an extra place at the table. I am *divorced.* My life is here, albeit alone. I will let go of the thought of moving back to Detroit. Charlotte rocks. I love it here – most of the time. My kids love it here. And I will learn to love being a divorced woman here! Who knows, one day maybe Mark, the boys, and I will have Passover dinner together again. It could happen. One day.

And you know what? I am over the snow globes. I'm going to start my very own collection of perfectly-pretty, shiny things. Maybe diamond stud earrings? Or sparkly shoes!

Out with the old – and in with the new!

BACK IN THE SADDLE

I'M SORRY,
I CAN'T TONIGHT.
I'M BUSY. I HAVE DATES.

I mean, a date. A date. Remember that? I know, it's been forever since you've been on one. But you can do it. You have to get back on that horse, and ride it! Come on! Dating is amazing. And this one is cuter than last night's. And funnier. And smarter (I think.) Wait... maybe not. Shit. What's his name again?

When it rains, it pours y'all. And let me tell you, it pours *hard*. It's raining men! Amazing, hot, smart men. I'm singing in my head. And no, I didn't write my digits on the bathroom wall, or wake up last week and decide to start "serial dating." It just happened. I started getting asked out. And I don't know why, or how. OK, maybe I joined Tinder. And, in carpool, the guy I've been crushing on asked for my number. Maybe, just maybe, I got fixed up with a nice Jewish guy in Charlotte. Be still my beating heart! You see, I was putting that "I'm ready" energy out there....

I am single.

I am divorced.

I am ready.

There's like this insane double standard that rules the world, and I've about had it. Men have it all. Men can do whatever they want. Men can go out with multiple women at the same time and it's fine. But the minute a woman decides to accept more than one date, she's a slut. Well, I am no slut, and I'm not lonely. Nor am I trying to fill a void. I'm not hungry and looking for a free meal. Jesus! What do you think, I'm "dating for dinner?" No, I am just dating. Getting to know new people. Not to find the "one." I'm trying to find a guy who I dig. And if it ends up being more, well then, cool. What is wrong with that? I am not afraid of being alone, in fact, I like it. I was married for thirteen years! And, it's my turn to have some dating fun. It's my turn to feel wanted. It's my turn to *be* wanted.

THERE, I SAID IT AND I'M NOT TAKING IT BACK.

Here it comes though, the sob story. So if you don't want to hear it, stop reading. But it's where as women, and mothers, we can all relate. Actually, men too. I think men want to be wanted as much as women. Don't you, guys? I won't leave my male readers out. Married, single, or divorced, we're all searching for affection, and longing for intimacy. Don't we all want to be wanted?

I JUST WANT TO BE WANTED!

But let's go back for a minute, shall we?

I lived for 12 years talking to kids. About kids.

I lived for my kids.

I wanted to shower – but stayed in sweatpants all day. I pumped my boobs. I got drooled on, climbed on, peed and spit up on (not to mention occasionally pooped on). My hair was in a ponytail. And like most couples, when Mark and I went on a date, we had high hopes! I wanted to stay out past 9 pm, and drink wine – whoop it up! We'd get a sitter and go out for a romantic dinner, but our conversation went right to the kids. But that was marriage. And life. And I was mostly happy. I loved being a mom, and a wife. But I missed being a *woman*. I felt lost and sad. My "pretty" was gone. And my sexy was lost somewhere between the diaper pail and the dishwasher.

But thank goodness for meds. (Yes, I take them.) And so does most of the Free World so give me a break. If you're reading this, and you don't take something, maybe you should. Life is too short to be miserable. If you are depressed, really, see your doctor – you could actually be happy! Treat your kids better, be nice to your husband (or ex). What's wrong with choosing happiness? I choose happy. And if pills make me happy, fuck it. I am not ashamed. I took them when I was married, and I will probably take them for the rest of my life. Ain't no shame in my game. Look, I would never be able to deal with the assholes around me if it wasn't for my 150 mg. of

Wellbutrin. Oh, and trust me, the assholes would never be able to handle me unmedicated. Ha!

I AM A MEDICATED MOMMA!

But since my divorce, I've had a lifestyle change if you will. My babies are grown up, my tits are brand spankin' new (thanks, Mark), my fat is gone, and I'm left with only a nice Frankenstein-like scar across my stomach that looks like I was cut in half by one of those whack-job magicians on a bad day (tummy tuck). I actually feel confident. Not *cocky*, but confident. I know who I am, what I want, and what I don't want, and I have no problem sharing it. I know what I'm doing in bed. And I know how to tell a man what I want. I won't settle for anything but delicious, yummy sex. I am forty-ish, and I'm in my prime. Finally, I can have sex when I want, how I want, and with whom I want!

I LOVE SEX – AND I'M NOT AFRAID TO HAVE IT.

Let's do this thing! I'm ready to conquer the world! I am woman, hear me roar. But listen guys, we need you to pay the bill on the first date. Damn straight. You pay that fucking bill or you are out. What kind of guy doesn't pay the bill on the first date? I'm telling you, they exist. And I swear, they are all going out with me. What the hell? I mean, it's not like I'm a diva, but it's a nice first date gesture. On the other hand, I had a guy open the car door for me the other night. I was like, *nice*.

It's amazing what doing your hair and wearing a cute outfit can do for a girl. Not to mention the fact that the guy says something about how you look. It's nice to hear, right? But it's more about how I *feel*. And how he looks at me when I'm talking. And he actually wants to know about me. *He really wants to hear about me.* We laugh and touch and he thinks I'm funny. I flip my hair and smile. You might think it's pathetic. But try it on a Saturday night with your husband. Meet at a restaurant and pretend he's a blind date. Don't talk about your kids or your bills. Go out for a nice dinner and flirt. See how great your sex is that night. Bet it's hot!

I haven't forgotten I have and love my kids. And I miss them on my off-weeks. And I do volunteer work and laundry and clean the house and all the same shit every other woman does. But now I'm also doing stuff for me, as well. I'm finding myself. I work out. And I write. And I sleep in. But guess what? I'm single now and I go out when my kids are with their dad. And I flirt. I get to think about someone else besides my husband — and not feel bad about it! Are you jealous, ladies? Don't be haters; live vicariously through me if you want.

And if you're happily married, I applaud you. And I'm the jealous one.

Being happily married is the hardest thing in the world. It's work and you can't ever give up. Most of my married friends have wonderful, strong, beautiful relationships. And others are full of shit. They should have thrown in the towel years ago, but they're scared to be alone. And, they don't want to give up the country club lifestyle and deal with what they'll get.

Good thing for vibrators. And wine. *OMG, did she just say that?* Yes, I did. And I'll say it again over and over.

For now, my only goal is to be "happily divorced." I'm going to date, have fun, and enjoy being single. If you're divorced, that should be a healthy and safe part of your plan, too. Being alone isn't a bad thing! It's all part of the process. Take the time you need to get your wits about you. Enjoy feeling wanted again. Don't feel pressured to jump right into a committed relationship. Trust me, if you jump, it will end as quickly as it started. And the pain will be far worse than you can even imagine.

THE PAIN OF THE FIRST "OUT-OF-THE-GATE RELATIONSHIP" WILL HURT WORSE THAN YOUR DIVORCE.

And do you want to know why? Hold on for this one, y'all. (And don't you dare get pissy.) *Because you actually didn't want this relationship to end.* I know. Unlike your marriage, you didn't want it to be over. You were prepared (or at least you had time to prepare) for your divorce. But this relationship? Uh, no. It sneaks up on you. And BAM! You. Are. Dumped. Fuck. And you actually liked the guy or girl. You liked the way he made you feel, the way she kissed you. The butterflies and the fireworks. Holy shit, it all felt good, even when it felt bad. Kinda like high school again, huh? I know, I get it. But trust me. Take your time healing and finding you again.

THE FIRST ONE PUTS YOU ON YOUR ASS FOR DAYS.

I didn't listen to my divorced friends. I read all the books, like this one. I did! But it's impossible to tell someone in the midst of it all. I didn't want to believe it. And guess what else? The men asking me out were on the prowl for women like me, women who were vulnerable, and alone. Newly separated women are the low hanging fruit, the fresh meat in the dating pool. And these single guys have been waiting for the insecure batch to crop up. Sad, but true. Men might not even know they're doing it! How can they possibly want to date a woman right out of a marriage? She can't possibly be in any position emotionally or mentally to date. She can't possibly be ready for *any kind of real commitment!*

ARE YOU PICKING UP WHAT I'M LAYING DOWN? HEY, I TOLD YOU THIS WAS BULLSHIT-FREE.

Are all men dicks? No, some men are really awesome. And some women just want to fuck and run; they're not all considerate of others' feelings. Look, it's the way we are wired. And this after-divorce world we are trying to navigate is rocky. In fact, it's a total shit-show! We're vulnerable, scared, and insecure. There is nothing wrong with wanting to be wanted. Just remember to keep your self-respect intact along the way, you need to keep your wits about you. And, remember the Golden Rule, otherwise known as the law of reciprocity or *karma.* She can be a bitch.

Others have feelings, too, so treat people how you want to be treated. I always think, what if this guy were Jonah or Zac? Would I want a girl treating them the way I'm treating him? I ask the guy, "Would you want someone disrespecting your daughter the way you're disrespecting me?" Trust me, if they have a girl, it will stop them in their tracks.

I was ready to date when I was ready to date. And I made huge mistakes. I dated psychos, liars, and losers. But hey, we all make them. And I don't beat myself up. Some mistakes will be bigger than others, but we learn and we grow. Then, we write books and share our shortcomings with the entire world in hopes that we will help others so they don't fuck up as badly.

How am I doing? Do you feel like getting back up on that horse yet? Giddy up!

THE HARDEST BREAKUP

I SAT THERE.

MY EYES FILLED WITH TEARS...

BUT I COULDN'T BELIEVE IT.

The sound coming out of his mouth was forming sentences, but it surely wasn't the truth. And it surely wasn't for me. There was no way he meant what he was saying. Things were going so well. I mean I had dated so many wrong guys. This one was right! *We were right.* Our relationship was so solid. How was this happening? I listened, and I tried to breathe. And wanted to kill him. Is it normal to reach into the phone and strangle a person? He was saying awful things. He was making the biggest, most idiotic mistake of his life and I wanted him to shut his big fat mouth. But he kept talking. Why was he still talking? Didn't he know I was on the other end of the line and he was hurting me?

BUT HE SAID HOW HE FELT.

And although I felt hurt, sad, angry, I listened. Then I yelled and freaked out. Yet, there was nothing I could do. He felt what he felt. I tried to convince him I was his best choice. I was the one for him. And we texted back and forth for hours, saying hurtful, mean things. It was not my best day. In fact, it was one of my worst since the divorce.

I'm sorry for some of it, well most of it. But it's impossible to control what is out of my control. I can't control a person's emotions.

I can, however, control mine.

React to his actions, right? But fuck it's hard. Did you know in dating it's OK, even encouraged, to tell the other person if you're still in love with your ex? It's actually allowed? When you're dating and divorced you can sort of "cheat" and it's like not really "cheating." Fuck. He talked to her while we were together. She called him; she wanted him back. They actually met for lunch, and had coffee. Wowza. Who knew?

I DID KNOW ONE THING; I WAS NO LONGER WANTED.

A feeling I remembered far too well. Being unwanted, unloved. Wanting someone but getting nothing in return. I had a lump in my throat, tried not to cry. I remembered how I'd promised myself I'd never be in this position again. Ever. He was in still in love with another woman, and it was all I needed to hear.

I am better than this and I'm no one's second choice.

Ultimately, he did care about me. He wasn't saying our

time was a waste. I just wasn't the right one, I guess. She came back into his life, and he chose her. Do I like it? Fuck no. But we had no bonding commitment, we just dated. It's fucking dating! And divorced dating can be shitty, because this stuff *is* shitty. You get thrown these curve balls. Guys can leave, women can decide they are moving on. My poor kids. Shit. *My kids.* And his girls. I loved his girls.

I'll never introduce another man to my children until there's a ring on my finger. Which will be never. I am clearly taking a break after this one.

My ego was fried. My heart crushed. I felt like a loser. A fool. Shit, this hurt worse than my divorce. Why did a breakup with a guy I'd only known for a few months hurt more than my divorce from my ex-husband, the man I'd been married to for 12 years?

BECAUSE I WASN'T READY FOR IT; IT WAS AN UNWELCOME SURPRISE.

I didn't ask for it, and I didn't want it. There was no discussion. One day it was great, the next — poof! I felt stupid thinking we were on the same page. How could I have been so wrong? How could I have been so naive to think we were feeling the same thing? One day, we're on the boat with his girls. The next, I'm dumped for the ex-girlfriend I never knew he had.

That's divorced dating, y'all.

I lost a best friend — and an fantastic partner. He and I clicked; he got me. We laughed, and did stupid shit. I fell in love with his kids. And my boys loved him; he filled an empty place in my heart. And he was a good soul, a wonderful father, and a solid person. And I had my plus one again. We spent our time alone, together. I loved it. I loved having someone to do things with and go places with. I will miss that part of us. The "us" part of us. Did he make a huge mistake? Hell yes.

The worst part was hearing this shit, "Another one, Hurvitz?" or "Jesus, Jen... you're racking them up!" I hated it. As if I *wanted* to be dumped. Like I asked for men to treat me like shit. I have zero control over people's actions. If I'd had my druthers, I would have stayed with this one forever. He was a keeper. So, please give me a break. I'm just a girl trying to find a kick-ass guy. I don't really feel like dying alone.

Or watching football alone on Sundays.

I like sharing my ice cream, too.

He did send a nice post-breakup text. My heart dropped. He's a really good guy. I hope he's happy with the other girl and I hope she treats him right. She will, for a while. Then she won't again. They broke up for a reason. And in a week, I'll be dating someone else. In fact, I have a date tomorrow night! I always say, the best way to get over someone is to get under somebody else! Wow, I just realized this time, I was the "somebody" else. I feel used. He used me to get over her!

Awesome. I guess.

Oh well, it was a fun couple of months. I got to fly in a plane, shoot a gun, and fall in like. Now, if I can just stop thinking about him — and his cute smile. And awesome legs and how he kissed.

HEY! WHO IS FREE TONIGHT? DRINKS ON ME!

DATING ISN'T CHILD'S PLAY

SCENARIO 1: YOU'VE BEEN DATING A GUY FOR SIX MONTHS.
OK, FOUR MONTHS, THREE WEEKS, FIVE DAYS, AND THIRTY MINUTES.
BUT WHO'S COUNTING? YOU THINK HE'S GREAT.

He's funny — and smart. He calls when he's supposed to, texts you goodnight and then good morning. He's met your friends, and they like him! You've deleted the Tinder app. You think this is the real, drama-free relationship you've been seeking. But now the big question:

SHOULD HE MEET THE KIDS?

My stomach flipped. I actually felt a little nauseated. Remember me, your author? I'm getting over a big breakup where my boys met the guy? I can only go by experience. My own experiences. Look, we live and we learn and then we share what we think we have all figured out. Are you ready?

No fucking way! It's too early.

Keep that man all to yourself! Date and be adults. Live it up. Caveat: unless you and he are planning on being in each other's lives forever, do not do the kid meet. And you both need to feel it. Not just in your fantasy, he needs to feel it, too. I know, it's kinda harsh! But hear me out.

UNLESS THE PERSON YOU ARE DATING IS A "FOREVER AND ALWAYS" IN YOUR LIFE, DON'T MAKE THEM A "SOMETIMES AND MAYBE" IN YOUR CHILD'S.

You are an adult, it's hard enough for you to understand a breakup. You go through the pain and sadness. And sure you recover, slowly. Can you imagine how your child feels? Especially if they have formed a bond with the person? They are, no matter how well adjusted they seem — and I want you to read this sentence twice — still adjusting from the divorce, I guarantee it!

Look, I did it. I watched my boys ride the emotional roller coaster. No kid should relive the feelings of loss, recalling and reminding them of the divorce. I made this mistake more than once — and my boys are proof. My 12-year-old told me, after my last breakup, "Mom, you need a break until you can find a guy that stops lying." Nice, huh? They get it and they want us to be happy, not nauseated from a roller coaster of emotional overload.

We all believe in putting our kids first, wanting what's best for them. So, do what's best. Be unselfish and leave the dating to the grown-ups. They don't need to meet every Tom, Dick, and Harry that pops into your Bumble box. I'm looking for a new partner for me, not a new dad for my boys. I don't need to see if he gets along with my kids as a "litmus test." If he's the right one, then he will be a good parent to his kids. Share picture and tell stories about them. Unfortunately, as we all know, many post-divorce relationships end not so "happily ever after."

REMEMBER: NOT PESSIMISTIC, REALISTIC.

So, unless there is a ring on my finger, my kids will be getting me and only me. When I'm with them, it's quality us time. And when they're with their dad, I can date all I want — or not. No man is as important as my kid's emotional well being. Not anymore! I have screwed up too many times, and I won't do it again. And if the next guy I date finds it a problem, then he's not the one for me! Hmmm. I think I'll put that on my Match.com profile.

"Single Mom, not looking to blend families — ever!"

REALLY SAFE SEX

LET ME GET THIS STRAIGHT.

YOU PUT THIS DISSOLVING VAGINAL
CONTRACEPTIVE FILM IN YOUR VAGINA WHEN? OMG.

NOT MORE THAN THREE HOURS BEFORE,
OR LESS THAN 15 MINUTES PRIOR TO INTERCOURSE.

WTF ARE THEY TALKING ABOUT?!

Holy crap! I have a college degree, people! I have choreographed major dance numbers with hundreds of kids. I have climbed Masada. I have a reasonably high IQ. I should understand when to insert a piece of contraceptive film up my vajayjay! Come on, give a girl a break. Throw a girl a bone.

Wait.

Did you know you can actually buy vibrators now at Target? OK, off subject. But really, next to the condoms and the vaginal contraceptive film are teeny-tiny little vibrators. And cock rings! And I bought both. Tar-jay is not just for school supplies, ibuprofen, and tampons anymore.

Who knew?

I'm sitting at dinner and I look at my watch. It's almost three hours before I might get laid. "Might" being the operative word. And my date is hot. Ya, sure, I like my sushi, too. I'm enjoying the conversation. He has good teeth, great manners. Hmmm. Do I excuse myself to the Ladies' room and shove in the Vaginal Sperm Killer? Do I wait a bit longer? I mean, I do have two hours and forty-five minutes left and what if I don't want to sleep with him? OK, he's still talking. He's cute, I guess. I love this wine. Crap. I'm getting a bit tipsy. What if I can't figure it out? What if I rip the film, or it dissolves in my hand? This is awful! The clock is ticking. We get the check. I only have a half-hour! I am freaking out. I have to get that shit up in me like now! Drive faster, moron! Hurry. OK, great. Surely we'll have fifteen minutes in the house before... Phew, dog, move it! I'm in the bathroom. It's in. Game on.

I am safe. Right?

Why is this so difficult? Isn't being newly-single at 40-something hard enough without making safe sex dang near impossible? I have been having sex for the past 13 years with the same man for fuck's sake. The same penis. The same size. The same shape. The same semen! No worries. No diseases. No issues. And now, it's all I worry about. Where has this guy been? With *whom?* How many times? Am going to get knocked up? (Because yes, I am still fertile so, yes, I'm not that old!)

And the diseases, they're scarier and different, too. It's not your run-of-the-mill herpes anymore. And there's still bacterial vaginosis, chlamydia, and the old standby, gonorrhea. But have y'all heard of HPV? Ya, that sucker means business. Different strains of HPV cause different issues. And men can be infected, too. Oral cancers, cervical cancers. Scares the shit out of me. Scares the fun right out of having sex.

Ok, maybe not quite.

But happily divorced also means *healthily* divorced. And I'm your girl, OK? Read on, I've got you covered. Pun totally intended. OK, bad pun... but you'll thank me later.

When I got separated, I headed straight to my gynecologist for a full-body check. And I came out clean as a whistle. But, since I'd be getting back in the game, or saddle or whatever, my doctor recommended I be vaccinated for HPV or Human Papillomavirus. Not only is the virus nothing to sneeze at, the vaccine is also a doozy. I got shot up with a series of three shots in the arm over a six-month period. Ask your doctor. Look, all I know is I couldn't lift my arm for days!

But that pain was a good thing. Every time I thought about putting a condomless penis near my vagina, I'd get a sharp, shooting pain in my deltoid. And insurance doesn't cover the HPV vaccine, but gals... it's worth it. Unless you trust every person you sleep with, and every person they have slept with (yeah, do that math!), I say don't risk it. Get the vaccine.

Back to my story....

So, I come out of the bathroom, and try to act all normal, with this piece of film rolled in my hoo-ha. And I can't stop thinking about it. The four corners of it, I swear they are poking my insides, even though they're not. I'm a total loser. But what if he can feel it? Or even worse, he can taste *it?*

Shit. I need to get it out. I need to wash it out of me! How do you remove a Vaginal Contraceptive Film? Help! I think it's burning. I'm on fire. I'm having an allergic reaction. The lining of my vagina is peeling off and I need to get out of here, now! And we start to kiss and he's all over me. I jump up and scream, "I need to go home! I think I left the iron on!" It was the first thing that popped into my stupid burning-vagina head.

I never saw him again. (And my vaginal walls are fine, thank you very much.) I clearly overreacted. Newsflash: "Jewish girl overreacts and doesn't own an iron." Duh. In fact, once when I was still married, we took the kids on vacation. We stayed at a motel in Savannah and Zac opened the closet door, and screamed, "OMG, Mom! The room comes with a surfboard!" A "surfboard" because the child had never seen an ironing board. Never even seen one. That's how much I could have left the iron on.

But this dating shit has to get easier. Doesn't it? I mean, eventually, I will be able to figure it all out, right? The sex, the dating, the men. Oh, my!

Someday, I'll find a guy who has been snipped (a.k.a. had a vasectomy) — and who is squeaky clean. I'll put that on my dating profile: "Single Female seeks Single Male, must be sperm-free and disease-free. Please provide certified doctor's note on first date. Romantics encouraged." Ha ha! And next time I'm at Target, I'll pick up a box of condoms instead of a new cock ring. The Vaginal Contraceptive Film can stay on the shelf — right next to the tiny vibrators. I've had enough plastic, too! I mean, come on! I'm single, y'all! Aren't toys for married women? They were in *my* house.

I never want to see a fake, plastic dick again.

So, guys, I know you think it's hot to ask if I have "toys." Well, I don't. (Ok, maybe I do.) But I don't want them near me anymore. And I bet most other girls feel the same way. Why would we want a fake penis, when we can have the real deal? After years of being with our cold, plastic playmates, why would we choose fake over you? Be flattered. And maybe, just maybe, if you're really sweet, we will surprise you on a rainy day. Maybe I could have used mine to get that fucking contraceptive film out of my vag. OMG, that would have been the best idea! Why didn't I think of that? It would have been a win-win.

ONLY THE REAL DEAL FROM HERE ON OUT.

Well, real and covered in latex. Snipped, disease-free, and covered in latex. Isn't being happily and healthily divorced fun?

WHAT MEN REALLY WANT

SO, IT'S ALL GOOD.
THIS DIVORCE THING IS GOING GREAT.
MARK AND I ARE FRIENDS, OK?

And it's his birthday, and I feel like you should know. And it's not like I'm not baking a cake, but I thought about it. So for his birthday, I'll give him a shout out. A big old birthday shout out for my ex-hubby, Mark. Happy Birthday! There. Now I'm done, and I don't feel like I have to go on anymore, or buy him a gift. But I do have to get him something from the kids. And if you are divorced, or separated, you should do the same thing. Always. It is your job to get a gift or card for your child to give to your ex on birthdays and holidays. Yes, it is. Yes. It. Is.

Kids don't have cars, or money, so as a divorced parent, it's your responsibility to buy the ex a dang gift. Don't fuck that up. The only one hurting in this situation is the child.

I hope you see that. You do know that if they celebrate a birthday and your kids don't have a present for Dad or Mom, they will feel like shit. And it will be your fault.

So, what would Mark want? I know what I want *for* him. A girlfriend. That's right, it's my goal in life to find Mark the "perfect mate." I would be so happy if I could pick his next wife. I want her to be smart, pretty, nice to my kids, kind, and a little on the plumper side. Is that too much to ask? I'm kidding, of course. Hopefully, she will like me. I want to be friends. I think it's easier if we can hang out. So, it's only fair that she shouldn't be hotter than me.

OH, AND SHE HAS TO BE OK HAVING ME IN MARK'S LIFE, BECAUSE I'M HERE TO STAY.

I am on the case and doing major research, and by "major research" I mean going out for drinks with my guy friends. Nice, right? Hey, I'm getting their view on women and relationships. The good, the bad, and the ugly on dating and divorce. From a male's perspective. Now, this may not be hardcore scientific fact from university studies, but this is some good shit. Out of the mouths of real men! Beer-drinking men. Scotch-drinking men. Loose-lipped men telling it like it is.

OK, so I talked to maybe ten guys. And we were drunk. And I sort of remember some of what they said, kind of... but OMG it was a fun night! And honestly, this book is all about relatable stories, so, here's what I have. I think it's really good. These guys gave me honest feedback that I'm compelled to share with women who want to know exactly what men want. Are you ready? Some of this may sting, but remember, I love you. And truth be told, I fell victim to these faux pas myself.

NO PETS ALLOWED. Do not post an online dating site picture of you with your dog. Or cat. Or parakeet. Or snake. Or, for the love of God, your ferret. Do not pose with it, kiss it, or dress it in a Halloween costume. You are trying to get a man not get sent away for a "rest." He can find out how crazy you are later.

IF IT QUACKS LIKE A DUCK. Do not pose with a "kissy-face." This is also known as "duck face" where you suck in your lips in a pseudo-pout, and unless you're fourteen and just discovered Snapchat, it's a big "no." He doesn't want to kiss a duck. Do you understand? Smile. Show your pretty teeth, bright eyes, and smile. Now, I'll admit, it happens to be my favorite online dating pose, but I have a man. All the men I've talked to hate the anorexic, heroin-chic sucky-face. You are not fourteen and you are not one of the Olsen twins. Save the pout for up close and personal.

PICTURE THIS. Stop with the selfies – or learn how to take them. If you must post a selfie online, don't hold the camera so high that you're forehead is in another time zone. Put the phone in front of your face. Or ask a friend to take some pictures of you, or post recent pictures of you doing something you love. The next time you meet someone for coffee or go for a walk with a friend, snap a pic. Lose the selfie.

BAYWATCH. Never, and I mean never, post a picture of yourself in a bikini on a boat. Or a beach. Or standing in your bathroom looking in the mirror. Do not post any picture of you half-naked! You are setting yourself up. Even if that's the best shot you've ever taken, and the best you've ever looked, you know he will be comparing you to it forever. And, you will attract a shit-ton of tire kickers. Do you really want all those guys who just want a bikini babe? Keep your clothes on. At least until you meet him.

COCK OF THE WALK. Don't post pictures of you with your brother, or dad, or a professional baseball player you once dated. No, OK? A guy doesn't want to think of you with another man, even if it is your "gay best friend from LA." Keep the men out of your life, and in the past. It's all better left unseen. Skeletons in the closet, ladies.

SILENCE IS GOLDEN. Make conversation. Speak. And not only when spoken to, OK? These are modern times, gals. Sure, men like to talk, but they also, if they're doing this right, want to hear about you. I had a guy tell me he went on a date with a girl who said "yes" to everything he said. Finally he said, "Do you want to go home and fuck?" She said, "Yes," without even realizing it. She wasn't even paying attention. He took her home and dropped her off. Date fail.

CHECK, MATE. Offer to pay the bill. Yes that's right, offer no matter what. First date, second date, any date. Just offer. That's all he wants you to do. It's sweet, and kind.

And chances are, he won't ever take you up on it. But by offering you show three things:

1. You're secure
2. You're confident
3. You are one sexy bitch.

PUT A RING ON IT

IT'S JUST A RING.
MY ONLY REAL BLING.
MY ROCK.

The shiniest, prettiest, most beautiful thing I have ever owned.

But really, it's a *thing*.

Mark texted me, "You should sell your engagement ring." He knows I'm buying the rental house, so I could use the cash. I am buying my very own house. Pretty cool, huh? Scary-cool. My own property. Mark's trying to help; I get it. But it made me sad, it's the finality of it all. I took it off two years ago, sure, but to sell it? Wow. What if Jonah or Zac want it someday, or what if I want to give it to my niece? Or use the diamond for a necklace? Sell it?

It's just so — final.

I'm not sad as much as I actually feel guilty. Like, it isn't really mine to sell. I'll ask Mark if he wants to split the profit. He did buy it after all, right? Or maybe I should sell it, and put the money into the kids' college fund. Or go to Israel or back to Italy with them. It doesn't seem right to sell it. Maybe if we hated each other, it would be easier. I could go on a shopping spree, or get my tits redone. It's definitely time for a new pair! Even the fake ones start to sag after gravity gets ahold of them.

I'm looking at the text back from Mark. He says, "Nope. It's yours. Take the money and go back to school." So, I reply, "OK" and continue like it was all good. Where should I go to get the most money for it? Blah, blah, blah. Meanwhile, I'm sobbing. I can barely see the fucking screen on my iPhone. I'm sitting in my car, looking down at my old engagement ring, crying like a baby.

I didn't expect to sob like a hormonal teenager in my car, but I did. This divorce thing ain't easy, y'all. It's a roller coaster, and anyone who tells you differently is a liar. Or on a really high dose of Prozac. Much higher than mine.

I THINK MOST OF THE TIME, I LIKE WHERE I AM.

But then out of nowhere, something gets me, pulls the rug out from under me, and knocks me on my ass. And it doesn't mean I'm not over my ex. Or that I'm not ready to date, or have a new boyfriend. Please. It means at that exact moment, I'm hurting. That's it. Nothing more, nothing less. Don't read into it or get your panties in a bunch. It comes with the territory.

Then I remember, I've got this. I am where I am meant to be. Fuck it. I'm going to sell my engagement ring, and put myself through school! I deserve it. And who knows, maybe I'll get another ring one day. Hell, I'd even take a Ring Pop! Remember those? I loved those dang things. Strawberry flavored. Diamonds are overrated, Ring Pops only cost a buck! Life was so much easier then when all I wanted was a Ring Pop. I'd give just about anything for "easy" right now.

What happened to life just being simple?

Do you ever feel that way?

Sometimes getting out of bed in the morning is all you can do. It is your daily activity. I feel that way sometimes. I stay in bed some days and stare at the ceiling, hoping my life will change, or something fabulous will fall out of the sky. But then, I take a deep breath, and I look at my ankle. Oh, I have this wicked tattoo on my left ankle. I got it before we moved to Charlotte. When my ex decided to uproot us and bring us down South, he told me it would be for a year. "One year, Jen. Come on! Then we can go back home." Six years later I'm sitting here, sobbing and divorced. Funny, huh? But I thought getting the tattoo was better than popping Xanax. It's Hebrew, the tattoo. And even though I have no clue how to read it, I know it says, "Neshamah" which in English means to "breathe in the soul." Or just breathe.

Kind of perfect.

I love it, even though it's totally not me. I'm like a firecracker! And breathing is so not my thing. But it couldn't be more appropriate under the circumstances. It does exactly what I need it to do; it serves its purpose. I look at my tattoo and I breathe. I slow down. I focus and center my shit. I realize that I can do whatever it is I'm freaking out about. I just have to chill out and relax. Not my favorite words to hear! Mostly because I'm not good at doing any of them. And I find them to be condescending: being told to "calm down," "chill out," "relax," (that one really gets me!) and "breathe." I mean, who wants to be told to do those things when in the middle of a meltdown? Like when in the history of being told to "calm down" has a woman actually, in fact, ever calmed down? Not me. In fact, if a guy says any of the above, I usually get even more amped-up!

But it is true. We need to do them all; I need to do them. For my boys — and for my sanity. Life is not always going to be easy after a separation or divorce. Today was one of the lowest points I've had in a long time. But no more crying! I looked in the rearview mirror. What a mess! I wiped my face and put on some gloss. Fuck it. I'm going to sell the ring. And who knows, maybe I'll give the money to Autism Charlotte. Or split it between the boys for their college funds. Or open a dance studio. So many options! But for right now, I am just going to sit here and breathe. And then go buy a Ring Pop. I hope they have strawberry.

A PRINCESS AND A PORNSTAR

READ AT YOUR OWN RISK.

THIS CHAPTER IS "R-RATED."

EITHER SHUT THIS DOWN NOW,

OR HANG ON TIGHT.

'm giving you fair warning, this is not for the "Gasp! Did she really just say that"-ers! This is for the, "Bitch, please I feel the exact same way"-ers! So, let's get this show on the road, shall we?

I am perturbed. Perplexed. Downright bewildered! I just can't take it. I am in one of the biggest conundrums of my post-divorce life! I feel ashamed. And dirty. And like I'm doing something wrong. But am I really? You be the judge.

I WANT TO BE TREATED LIKE A PRINCESS, BUT FUCKED LIKE A PORNSTAR!

Wow. That wasn't so tough. (That was easy, actually.) But what *is* hard is getting respect from a guy, without acting like a nun. If we have a connection and I feel like sleeping with him on the first date, then dammit, I will! Why does that make me a whore? Worse, why do I *feel* like a whore? I still deserve to be treated with kindness. I can talk dirty, *and* be sweet. And I can look nice — and want to act naughty!

I want to be told I'm pretty. And yes, I want my door opened for me. And yes, please pay the check on the first date. And yes, I'm smart. Of course I'm a good mom; can you even remember I have kids? And I have a job, I'm a writer. And not just raunchy stuff, but heartfelt topics, too! I get it, it's confusing. There is a fine line between what's appropriate and what's not. Especially when females are so confident and strong-willed these days. We are sexy, but tricky. We demand respect, but we can be in-your-face. Trust me, I wouldn't want to be a guy in today's dating world.

I'm just saying it's not easy getting respect with online dating. But I'm not about to sacrifice who I am to get it. I am outgoing and personable. Some might see me as suggestive. I guess I like sex. And what's wrong with that? Everyone likes sex, they just don't say it in a blog (or a book). Most of you keep it to yourselves. But, behind closed doors... you little sneaks!

A PRINCESS AND A PORNSTAR. PERFECTION!

Why can't we be both? I say we can. Is it my issue, or his? I think most men would agree, they want a woman who is classy in the boardroom — and sultry in the bedroom. And when I do find the right guy, he will get it. He will totally understand my princess and the pornstar thing, and he will respect me for the woman I am. He will treat me like a princess in public. And, he will fuck me like a pornstar wherever we decide to do it, bedroom or otherwise! Ha!

I THINK I'M CONTAGIOUS

DO I SMELL?

I DON'T THINK I DO. I MEAN, I WEAR DEODORANT.

IT'S BEEN FOUR YEARS SINCE MY DIVORCE,
AND THEY STILL WON'T TALK TO ME.

Clearly, I do not stink. It has to be something else. There has to be some other reason no one wants to be near me. I am cute, I'm smart, and I'm fun. Shit. I'm like so goddamn fun! And not only am I fun, but funny! And I think I'm a pretty good person, too.

SO WHY IN THE NAME OF ALL THINGS SOUTHERN, AM I STILL SUCH A SOCIAL OUTCAST?

Four years ago, I was happily married. I lived in a big, beautiful house in a big, beautiful subdivision, in big, beautiful Charlotte, North Carolina. It was all so big and fucking beautiful, I wanted to vomit. And I was happy. *Ish. Happy-ish.* And my kids were in a fabulous private school (still are), and we had dogs. We belonged to the country club. I was living the American Dream. I drove a Range Rover, played tennis, and (OMG I'm making myself sick) I got my nails done every week. I walked around town in my "athleisure-wear" even though I wasn't one bit active. I had coffee with "my girls." We went to "chef's dinners" at the Club with our husbands; I had the perfectly-perfect life. From the outside.

Then my glass house started to crack and Mark and I decided to separate and then divorce. And how my "perfect" life did change. What a shit show! I realized that I lost not only my husband and my children for half of their lives, but I also lost my friends. Suddenly, my "lunch ladies" didn't have time for me, and my tennis group was now full. And my married friends' husbands? They wouldn't let their wives near me! I might be infectious.

AFTER ALL, DIVORCE IS CONTAGIOUS, YOU KNOW?

If you look at the numbers, you'd think it was. I can't believe what an epidemic divorce has become. Good thing people keep writing books like this, huh? Before we know it, kids like mine will be in the majority at school, divorced parents will be the norm. Yikes. I wonder if there's a vaccine for this virus. (I kid. Kind of.)

I remember sitting on my shower floor sobbing, wondering if I was always going to feel this shitty. Well, it's been four years, and it still fucking sucks. My married friends still go out with all the married girls, and I'm sitting home binge-watching Netflix. And my ex is my closest friend. Crazy, right? Oh, but wait! I'm good for a lunch.

After the sun goes down, forget it. Divorced women, we are dangerous. If you give us alcohol, we turn into hookers. Something about the dark combined with a cocktail... careful, y'all, we might actually be too much fun!

And girls' trips? Forget it! I'm never invited with the married girls anymore. In fact, I was replaced by another married friend. Damn that hurt. Social media kills me. I feel like a teenager with hurt feelings after seeing pictures of my "group" going to concerts without me. Or having birthday parties at the lake, and I'm not invited. My heart hurts. But honestly, what do I have to bring to the table? All I have to talk about are the hot dates I go on and the amazing sex I have. And what bars I frequent or my horrible relationship with my ex-husband. Wait, *what?* As you have read, we are best friends; he is my rock. Ours happens to be one of the most amicable divorces I've ever known. I think Mark and my friendship might make my old friends uncomfortable. Divorces are supposed to be horrible, right? It's like they don't know how to handle a healthy, happy one. It's almost "abnormal." Or too good to be true.

Or, maybe I know too much about their marriages? Maybe I make divorce sound too good. Maybe the grass looks a little greener over here? Hell, who knows. And who really cares. But I miss them, my girls. And my old life. Not the country club or and the house. Who needs that material shit? It's the friends I miss, the women who were a huge part of my world. They loved me when I was married, what's changed? It still hurts even four years later. But I guess it's part of being divorced, right? You lose the life you used to have — and the relationships you thought were solid. I sometimes wonder if I got engaged, or remarried... would they take me back? Sigh.

I am happily divorced, but lonely sometimes.

I am happily divorced, but I still get sad.

I am happily divorced, but I miss my old life.

I am happily divorced.

But I am not contagious! I'm not. I'm just single again. And it's hard, and not where I ever thought I'd be. Divorce is not a disease or something you catch. It was a choice I made, for my family and I'm happier now than I was in my marriage. So, listen up, y'all! I'm not a virus! I'm not going to infect you, and I'm surely not going to be the reason your wife jumps ship.

If you end up divorced, it's all on you.

But you can bet your sweet ass, I'll see ya on Tinder!

STAND BY YOUR mAN

WE BITCH.
WE COMPLAIN.
WE YAP AND WHINE.

Yet, we expect our men to hang around? OMG, ladies! What the hell is wrong with us? Wait, strike that. I need to change my pronoun. What is wrong with *you*? I am doing fine over here. I stopped that shit when I realized I lost my marriage by acting like a spoiled brat. It won't fly for long, my friends. That shit gets old real quick. Your men might last a good ten years or so, but then one day, you'll find out he's shtupping the yoga instructor. What? Are you surprised? You're a bitch and you emasculate him (without even knowing it) every chance you get.

But I'm going to help you. If you are not divorced yet, read this so you stay married. If you are divorced, read this to you keep your new man.

Whether you are married, dating, or in a long-term relationship, it's time to change your tune. Listen, I can help you keep your man. How, you ask? Well, I learned the hard way; I used to be that "bitch-of-a-wife." I was! OK, I'm not taking *all* the blame for my divorce. But it took work to realize I had a lot more to do with it than I chose to admit. Self-actualization is the key. Own it and fix it while you still have a chance.

But you do everything right! You do it faster and better. Your way is the only way. Am I right? *Wrong.* Back away! Let him do it *his* way. Every time you re-do what he's already done, it's like chipping away at a testicle. You might as well just take his balls and put them in your purse. "Honey, I have your testes, you can have them back next Tuesday." Jesus, is your relationship really worth re-packing that suitcase? It is fine the way he did it. Life will go on if he puts a white towel in with the darks. (Maybe?)

Let him open your car door (or pull out your chair, or pay the bill). I know, it sounds stupid! But men love to do it. It's sweet and chivalrous. I remember when I started dating my last boyfriend, I actually yelled at him for opening the damn door. "OMG, I can do it! What? You don't think I can get my own door?" I thought I was being feminist and strong. My divorce was just final and I wanted to prove I could do it "all on my own," even if it meant opening my own car door. Instead, I sounded ungrateful. So now, my new boyfriend opens the door every single time. And I let him. Oh, and I say, "Thank you, Baby."

OK, y'all are not going to like this one. Ready? *Ask for help.* I know, it's insane! Why would you ever ask a man to help you? Well, if you can believe this shit: men love to help us. They live for it. Trust me, they'll come running swords raised. So ask them. I never asked Mark, and you know what happened? I was always angry that he didn't help me. I would huff and puff around the house, resenting him. *Why isn't he doing the laundry? Why didn't he pick up dinner? Why the fuck can't he do the dishes, doesn't he see them in the sink?* Why didn't I just ask? Lesson learned. I'm divorced, ladies. Open your mouths and ask. And then say, "thank you."

Don't sweat the small stuff. Who cares if the shower door isn't closed all the way? Who cares if the towels aren't folded in an exact square? Who cares if he didn't wipe off the sink after he shaved? *Who cares?* Stop nagging. Life is too short to worry about mundane bullshit. And listen, if it really bothers you that much, do it your damn self. For real, just do it. Shut it and smile.

A real smile.

And stop resenting him because you did it and he didn't.

Just fucking smile.

You are nice to the mailman. The checkout lady at the grocery store gets a smile. You're a doll to the manicure chick. But when you get home to your man, the person you are supposed to love the most, you lose your happy. It's gone. Poof! And I get it! I do. My ex used to say, "Everyone in the world gets, "Happy Jen," except for me." How sad is that? And I never even realized I was doing it. Wasting all my "nice" on strangers, when my husband was the one who deserved it the most.

Have sex, make love, fuck like rabbits. If you want to stay connected it's the only way. Period. And I won't listen to any bullshit that says otherwise. Don't give me that crap that you can go for a month, and you're good. Or six weeks. Or you have friends that haven't had sex in a year and they are "just fine." They're lying. If you're sexless, you are not fine. Your relationship is not healthy, and you cannot be happy in it. Sex pumps pain-killing hormones called endorphins into your body, and it helps you bond by releasing the "love hormone" called oxytocin. And studies now show that having sex helps you live longer.

LADIES, FUCK YOUR MEN.
IF YOU DON'T, HE WILL FIND SOMEONE WHO WILL.

So, if you're saying, "Holy shit, this is me!" or "I could be writing this shit," don't worry. Check yourself, and change your behavior. Baby steps. When your man walks through the door tonight, thank him for working so hard all day. Kiss him, say you love and appreciate him. Ask him to help you with a few things, then snuggle up in bed and watch *Orange is the New Black*. You can keep your man! And don't forget to make love to him before y'all fall asleep. Oh, and do it with a smile!

I'm IN LOVE WITH MY EX

GOT YOUR ATTENTION, RIGHT?
CLEARLY, I HAVE SOME EXPLAINING TO DO.

After being divorced for almost five years, how can one say they're in love with their ex? Simple, I am. I love him more now than I did when we were married! I find him more attractive, sweeter, and a downright pleasure to be around. Oh, for fuck's sake, pick your mouths up off the floor and hear a girl out!

You've read the previous chapters, Mark and I have a unique but completely attainable relationship. It's not unheard of, or out of the realm of possibility. Anyone can do it! It is feasible to be in a productive, healthy un-family. But it takes effort to coexist, co-parent, and live separately, together. From early on, Mark and I have worked to make our divorce as amicable as it can be. I'm not going to sugarcoat it and tell you it's been easy or always fun. Hell no. We have had our tough times and shitty days.

BUT I LOVE MY EX-HUSBAND.

And although we may not be meant to be married, we got two amazing kids out of the deal. So when we decided to pull the plug and get happy, we also chose to do it right! It's about the kids. Being happily divorced is just as difficult as being happily married. I flat out love my ex and I'm not ashamed to say it.

HE KNOWS THAT A HAPPY LIFE MEANS A HAPPY EX-WIFE!

Life is like a song. Here are a few I could have really used looking back:

MO' MONEY, MO' PROBLEMS. It's always about the money, isn't it? And I don't mean the alimony and child support, y'all. That shit is what it is, legally. Listen to me. Don't fight over money or give it to attorneys. Keep it between you. It should all go to your kids in the end. It's all the same money! I didn't get that at first, but my ex was so good about explaining it. I was scared. Divorce is terrifying. I had no idea what I was doing after being married for 12 years. Whom do I trust? He kept saying, "We need to focus on the boys." And we did. We used a mediator and our money stayed ours. That's not to say you shouldn't use separate attorneys if need be. Some situations call for two independent lawyers. Do what best suits your needs.

WE ARE FAMILY. We are still a family, just in two different locations. We co-parent. Like really co-parent, we split everything fifty-fifty. And he is a better dad now than he was when we were married. The boys worship him because he is engaged 100% when they are with him. I've never seen them happier. And now after some time, we are able to have holiday dinners together. We sit together at the boy's basketball games, and we even took family pictures at our son's Bar Mitzvah. *The four of us.* Want to know why? Because one day, my kid is going to look back at his album and say, "My parents made the divorce easy. Look at my family."

SHE DRIVES ME CRAZY. He still deals with my crazy. Sure, he can hang up; I'm not his wife anymore. And most men would. They'd say, "You're so not my problem." But not my ex. He will text back every time. And he still does my taxes and fixes my leaky faucets. He will come over all hours of the night to catch mice. And he still listens when I'm spinning out over the stupidest shit. He's still my "go-to" when I'm upset about work, or even my boyfriend. I was his "crazy wife" and now I'm his "crazy ex." Anytime I need him, he's there. It's awesome. And all our friends think we are awesome and love our relationship. Some of them even say they wish their marriages were as happy as our divorce.

MY BOYFRIEND'S BACK. I know how to pick 'em. I pick losers. They seem to last about a month, maybe two. And my ex puts up with the aftermath. You know, me in bed for days, sobbing. Now, he insists on background checks before I agree to dinner. But, I'm finally dating a great guy! So, my ex and the boys gave him a nickname, "Number Thirteen." They named him Number Thirteen because they are sure he is the thirteenth guy I've dated. (Nice, huh?) But it's cool and we all get along. He actually showed up at Jonah's track meet wearing a #13 jersey. Ha! And, ready for this? We can all go to the pool, Mark on one side of me, Number Thirteen on the other, not a problem. Well, for us at least. My friends don't seem to know how to handle it. It's ok, everyone, we are all friends!

THE BITCH IS BACK. This song is my "ringtone" on my ex's phone. So, I guess I'm the reason he can't keep a woman? I kid. I am not the reason! Who wouldn't want to be with the greatest guy in town? What, because I'm all up in his shit? Please. All y'all should be happy we get along so well. It's a huge red flag when I'm dating a guy and he starts bashing his ex-wife. C'mon, it's not like he's answering my texts during dates anymore. (He stopped that years ago.) But yes, if a girl gets intimidated by me, forget it. She won't get far with the ex. I am a part of his life, even though I am not his loving wife. Get used to it, ladies. This bitch is here to stay! But truth be told, I'm just happy he changed my ringtone from Darth Vader's Imperial March.

So, if you ask my ex how he feels about me, what would he say?

"JENNIFER, YOU WERE HARD TO BE MARRIED TO, BUT ARE EASY TO BE DIVORCED FROM." – MARK WEINTRAUB, A MAN OF MANY WORDS.

I love it, and I love him. And there is not a man on this planet I'd rather be happily divorced from. Or happily raising our two amazing boys with.

AND SO THEY LIVED HAPPILY EVER AFTER DIVORCE (WITH NO BULLSHIT!).

REALITY BITES: DATING AFTER DIVORCE

I'VE DATED TALL GUYS.
AND NOT SO TALL GUYS. SMART MEN –
AND TOTAL FUCKING MORONS.
GOOD ONES, AND SOME, WELL, NOT SO GOOD.

Let's just say, over the past five years, I've run the gamut from turkey callers to pathological liars and I'm still here to write about it. I've learned a shit-ton about what I'm looking for in a relationship and I've grown along the way.

But let's be real here: being single isn't easy, or as fun as it sometimes looks. In fact, my best relationship is still with my ex-husband! We are happy. And no, We don't want to get back together. And yes, I actually have a great guy at the moment (this exact moment in time). But still, my ex and I are honestly the easiest relationship I've had over the last five years!

THE REALITY IS THAT DATING AFTER A DIVORCE TOTALLY BITES.

Well, it does! It's no secret, dating ain't like it used to be. But what are we going to do, sit at home and cry about it? Let our vaginas dry up and fall out? No, but we can bitch about it; bitching makes everything better. Or if you're as nuts as me, feel free to write a book about it. Here's a harsh dose of reality when it comes to dating after a divorce:

THE FIX-UP. When I got married at twenty-eight, I never thought another man (besides my husband) would ever see me naked. When I got divorced, I had to pay a fucking website to match me with a guy to see me naked.

REALITY CHECK: YOU WILL MEET YOUR NEXT DATE ON A SCREEN. What happened to getting fixed up by friends? Or meeting at a party? You think this shit is easy? Uh, no. Learning Mandarin Chinese would be easier. And I never thought I'd be meeting for coffee on a first date, discussing stuff like kid's activities and what our exes did to "fuck up the marriage." And no, I'm not going to meet a guy sitting at Starbucks. Please, I've been sitting at Starbucks for four years now. My ass is numb. It's all about the swiping, buzzing, and sexting. Can you make an emoji "blowjob?" If not, you're fucked!

THE VOCABULARY LESSON. Just when I thought I knew every word in the English language, I got divorced and started dating again.

REALITY CHECK: DATING NOW HAS ITS OWN LANGUAGE. With words like *ghosting, cushioning, breadcrumbing,* and *catfishing,* all new in my lexicon. Shit. And one of my favorites, a "THOT," which means: *that ho over there.* Nice, huh? And why do we need these new words? Well, it seems as we continue to screw up dating, we need them to explain why. Fabulous. Like *"cushioning"* for example. It's a newer term where a partner in a monogamous relationship continues to flirt with other people. If their main relationship fails, there's a backup plan, a cushion. Why do we need a new word for that? That's not cushioning it's called "cheating." There's already a word for it. I hope you're taking notes, there will be a quiz.

THE INTERVIEW. A little small talk, then the interview begins. He starts by rattling off a list of questions, which I brilliantly answer: Yes, I'm a Democrat. No, I don't like to sweat. I like my *own* kids, sure. Wait, let me redo number three. I answered it wrong! I clearly like kids. Who doesn't like kids? Fuck. I can see him making an imaginary check mark in his head (she doesn't like other people's children?). Dammit! OK, now it's my turn: What do you do, where do you live, and what do you drive? Wait! Don't leave, come back! What the hell! *Isn't that what all girls ask men on the first date?* No bitches, it is not.

REALITY CHECK: THINK BEFORE YOU SPEAK, YOU'RE NOT THE ONLY FISH IN THE SEA. Hell, you're not the only fish on his plate. He probably has a date after yours.

THE DATE. Chivalry is not dead, but boy has shit changed. It's 2017 and it's about time we stop expecting guys to court us like our in our parents' day. Pick your jaws up off the floor, girls.

REALITY CHECK: PRACTICE WHAT WE PREACH. EQUALITY. Men no longer feel responsible for paying every time. The first date, yes. But after that, you better reach for your wallet! Why should he pay all the time? What are you, a gold-digger? Well, that's exactly what it looks like if you sit on your hands, or run to the ladies every time the check comes. Look, divorced men have to pay alimony and child support. Many are supporting two households. Men will see your offer to pay as sexy and confident. *Expecting* a man to pay every time is obnoxious and unattractive (guys, thank me later).

THE PERFECT MATCH. OK, here's a shocker. Your one, your soulmate, your beshert? Guess what? He's probably not out there.

REALITY CHECK: FINDING THAT "PERFECT MATCH" IS SO MUCH HARDER THE SECOND TIME AROUND. Bubble burst? Pop! It was easier dating before you were married. All you had to worry about was which part of town to live in, and where to eat Passover dinner. Now, post-divorce, this is the United Nations. He wants to blend families, you don't. He wants to have kids, you're done down there. Your boys are off to college in a year, he has twins in nursery school — and a cat. You're allergic to cats and nursery schools. Even if you are bat-shit crazy in love, there is some external something that will fuck it up. It's torture! You may think you've found your next husband, and he tells you his kid schedule is Tuesday, Thursday, and every other Saturday, *the exact opposite of yours.* But you don't care. You'll try it anyway. Because you can fit a square peg in a round hole.

REALITY CHECK: YOU CAN'T FIT A SQUARE PEG IN A ROUND HOLE. THE UNITED NATIONS HAS INTERPRETERS. LOTS AND LOTS OF THEM. YOU DON'T SPEAK THE SAME LANGUAGE, ADMIT IT. Two years later you'll be calling me, saying, "You were right! She just didn't want kids! I thought she would change her mind." I promise, I won't say I told you so. But I'll be thinking it.

THE BREAKUP. Square peg, round hole. You make it fit. Sort of. Not really, but you spend months trying. And you will try desperately because you want something to work. *Anything* to work. Dating someone who isn't *exactly* right, is better than not being in a relationship at all, isn't it? No. It's called *settling*, people. And we all do it. But I learned it just prolongs the inevitable: a shitty breakup.

REALITY CHECK: YOU ARE SCARED TO BE ALONE. YOU CAN DO IT. WAIT FOR THE RIGHT PERSON. It took a lot of failed relationships to figure it out, but I won't date a guy that is kinda-sorta the one. I'd rather be alone. And maybe finding "the one" means waiting it out until the timing is right, like when your kids are in college and you can move to Alaska together. (Or a house in the mountains.)

REALITY NIBBLES. Look the reality is simple. Dating sucks balls. But when you are divorced, what other choices do you have? Rhetorical. You have to keep on going. So, maybe you find someone who fits *for now*. I'm not being snarky, really. If you do find a guy that *seems* to fit (most of the important boxes are checked), why not stay in the present? Enjoy what you have for now; stop worrying so much about the future. Can't we be happy being happy?

REALITY CHECK: ONE DAY AT A TIME, LIVE IN THE MOMENT.

LIVE IN THE MOMENT, AND JUST "BE" WITH THE PERSON WHO FITS FOR NOW.

There is not a thing wrong with having a "for now" person if you're honest about it. Be honest with yourself and your partner so no one gets hurt and your expectations are met. If one of you is looking to get married, and the other is never walking down that aisle again, "for now" isn't in the cards. Taking one day at a time is hard if you have a plan in your head, or you're looking for that "long-term relationship" that ends with spending every holiday together and blending families. But really, be smart. You just got divorced, or maybe it's been a couple years. Are you lonely? Is this person filling a void in your life? Does he check all your boxes, the really important ones?

REALITY CHECK: DATING SUCKS, YES, BUT BEING WITH THE WRONG PERSON IS WORSE. IT'S CALLED "SETTLING."

Oh, and for the record, I found the best guy. I got lucky; I'm in love. I'm not gonna go on and on, but he is the hip to my hop. The jam to my jelly. The zig to my za-*What?* Can't I be happy, but also be honest about how bad it sucked before we met? REALITY CHECK: I KNOW WE MAY OR MAY NOT BE TOGETHER FOREVER. But I'm having a kick-ass time finding out.

THE HAPPY ENDING

SO, HERE I AM.

I'M IN A FANTASTIC, HEALTHY RELATIONSHIP.

MY CHILDREN ARE IN A HAPPY PLACE.

AND MY EX IS PROBABLY GOING TO KILL ME (I KID)!

But all is good, and calm, and right. Mark and I are friends. Good friends, *really* good friends. I am tearing up as I type this, thinking about all we have been through to get to this point. We had to get divorced to be this happy. Or did we? I wonder sometimes if maturity would have helped us to get stronger together over time. If we had stayed together, could we have overcome some of our hardship? We will never know. But it's OK, we can't go back.

We just keep moving forward together, separately.

I love that. It's one of my favorite things I say to people. when they ask how the divorce has been, or if the boys are doing OK. I tell them, we parent the boys together, separately. Or is it separately, together? I guess it doesn't matter as long as we remain a team. We're on the same page, doing what's best for them. Always putting them first.

We are *happily divorced.*

And it's as difficult as being happily married. It takes work and patience. Understanding, and abandoning of egos. I know it's not easy, nothing that's actually worth having ever is. Fuck, this divorce should have killed me. The last five years should have killed me. The pain and sadness, the overwhelming loneliness. Some days, I was not even sure I would get out of bed.

IF YOU'VE GONE THROUGH A DIVORCE, YOU KNOW EXACTLY WHAT I'M SAYING. AND IF NOT, MAYBE I'VE HELPED YOU UNDERSTAND?

I still have hard days, sad days. But mostly they are good now. Every once in awhile one of the boys will ask, *"If you and Dad are such good friends, why can't you get back together?"* Yikes! It's confusing, to see Mark and me get along so well. And it has to be frustrating, too. If it's all so great, why aren't we a family? I tell the truth, we had to divorce to be this happy. If we went back to living under the same roof, chances are we would go back to the way we used to be. And while they don't always love that answer, it makes sense. They are both happy because we are happy. We did good, y'all. And I am proud of us.

WE ARE, ALL FOUR, HAPPILY DIVORCED.

During the more painful times, I began writing. To heal; it was purely cathartic. Then I realized my experiences were relatable and I could help others find a way to happiness. I felt better in the process. Maybe my stories would change just one woman's life. Or, maybe one man would be kinder to his ex. So, I started my blog, **The Truth Hurvitz,** which brought us here. Very few believed I could do it — actually write a book. Being a stay-at-home-mom. with no formal writing training. But not Mark, he knew I could do it. When I wanted to give up, he pushed me to keep going. For the boys and for me. I guess I have him to thank, huh? Thanks, Mark!

I was in an Uber car yesterday, coming home from a little jaunt to New York City. (Every Southern mommy needs a city-fix!) The driver asked me what I did for a living. I paused for a long moment, (looked down at my ankle), and with complete conviction I said, "I am a writer."

And for the very first time, I truly believed it.